INFP:
The Dating Bible of an INFP

By Lisa Ailers

Contents

INFPs are a rarified, sensitive bunch whose MBTI characteristics mark them as Introverted, Intuitive, Feeling and Perceiving. This is a unique (only a very small percentage of the entire population can call themselves INFP) and nuanced personality whose traits all merge together to form a creative, initially shy, yet oftentimes spontaneous individual who goes through life seeking fulfilling careers that make a difference — and romantic attachments that move them to their very cores. INFPs in love are dreamy yet understanding, and they know what they want without being single-minded in their pursuit of it.

But to fully wrap our minds around INFPs' prospects in dating and relationships, we have to comprehend the smaller parts that make up their whole, how their Introverted, Intuitive, Feeling and Perceiving aspects individually operate.

At the surface, Introverts seem like the kinds of people who would rather be at home, curled up in bed reading a good book, rather than out partying with a huge crowd of friends. In many instances, this is true, but it undercuts the real meaning of what an Introvert is. In fact, lots of Introverts enjoy active and busy social lives, but where they differ from their Extraverted counterparts is in the number of people with whom they prefer to interact and from where they draw their energy. First, Introverts may have acquaintances, but they always prefer to focus on — or "let in" — just a handful of select people. Second, Introverts are like singular batteries that need to be separate and alone to recharge their energies. They might even be the life of the party on New Year's, but you can bet they'll lie low for the rest of the week.

The Intuitive aspect is what gives INFPs their dreamy, idealistic qualities, their desire to create a better tomorrow, and their ability to think outside the box with both foresight and abstraction. Intuitives don't necessarily thrive on following their intuition, but INFPs do have a rather remarkable ability to read between the lines where both the written and spoken word are involved, as well as in interpersonal situations where a look can say more than a monologue. As positive as this trait is, INFPs can be prone to reading too much into what someone said and trying to find deeper meaning where there really isn't any.

Feeling types use emotion — their own and the feelings of others — as the basis for their actions. This is in sharp contrast to the more absolute Thinking types, who prefer logic and reasoning when it comes to making decisions at home, at work and in relationships. While Feeling types might encounter more bumps in their lifelong road toward fulfillment, they will find that all the experiences they accrue, both good and bad, serve to teach them about their own selves and the population in general. INFPs in particular use this knowledge to slide away from confrontation, whether it's discerning the best ways to avoid an unpleasant conversation or mediating between other parties to help bring them to a mutual resolution.

Perceivers are a hard-to-pin-down bunch. In school, INFPs might have been notable for their exquisite essays and works of creative writing (this personality type in particular tends to wield a literary pen with flair), yet the editor-in-chief of the school newspaper would have a difficult time getting them to turn their work in on time. It is ever so with the Perceiving INFP, who hates seeing his or her future plotted out down to the bathroom breaks and who resists ties that keep him or her under obligation. As much as that casual approach to life may rankle some (and INFPs can be dastardly procrastinators), Perceivers come with a built-in sense of flexibility and adaptability, so if a friend cancels plans at the last minute, they're hardly going to harbor any resentment over it. They'll simply call up someone else or decide to stay in with that new Netflix show — and be equally content.

There are other personalities, of course, that might have one, two or even three of these same aspects, but INFPs are unlike any other, and so they are uniquely calibrated to take on the world of dating and relationships in a way that is entirely their own. These four particular aspects combined in one individual make for a personality that is generous and spirited when it comes to sharing his or her life with others, yet quick to feel disappointment when the other party lacks those qualities that the INFP values. No INFP is perfect and there is no "perfect match" when it comes to other personality types, yet some clearly work better with the INFP than others, and it might surprise you which ones have the potential to last "until death do them part."

Here is the INFP matched up with the 15 other MBTI personality types. Every pairing has potential and nothing is written in stone, but this should give you greater insight into the matchups that could mean wedding bells or "turn and run like hell."

1. INFP and the ISTJ

Opportunity: If there is anything INFPs can gain from the opportunity to date the ISTJ, it is how to be more practical, logical and grounded. INFPs have a tendency to deal with the world the way they would want it to be and not how it truly is, while the ISTJ is a pragmatic realist with his or her two feet planted firmly on the ground, so mixing the two together could really open the INFP's eyes. And there might be few things that get the INFP to show up for a date on time, but chances are good ISTJs know just the right combination of words to strike a chord with their more flighty (and less responsible) partner — the type of verbal smackdown INFPs really need to hear now and then to remind them that others count on them and can be hurt by their actions, however innocent the intent.

Threat: In a perfect world, the INFP imagines that he or she could date anyone and be happy, but the hard reality is that the ISTJ — for all his or her Introversion, to which the INFP can relate but will not necessarily become a better person for having been exposed — is a terrible match, if not the very worst there is. Because both types would contentedly turn down dinner party invitations and instead stay in Saturday after Saturday, without anyone else present to guide their conversation, the two types would inevitably come to find that their world views rub against each other like two coarse bricks. Communication, in particular, would be the most troubled area, as the ISTP has little-to-no quandaries when it comes to issuing criticism, and the INFP tends to take even the slightest bit of critique to heart, internalizing and stressing over it or, worse, lashing out with irrationality (to which the ISTJ would respond with jarring emotionless calm).

Short-term Potential: That slippery substance known as chemistry or sex appeal cannot ever be discounted; an INFP's laugh could attract the glance of the ISTJ and an introduction might be made, followed by some rather surprising and out-of-character intimacy that can only be attributed to pheromones. As wayward as the INFP's life might seem, this is a type who tends to warm up to the physical aspects of relationships slowly, while the ISTJ is old-fashioned traditions personified. On the surface, they both want the same thing: a satisfying, long-term relationship built on trust and loyalty, and in the early months this desire could be enough to sustain a partnership (particularly if both partners are reaching an age when they feel as though they had better get married or they will die all alone). The novelty of being with someone who thinks so differently could, in particular, pique the INFP's interest long enough to make a short-term relationship stick.

Long-term Potential: Relationships take hard work, but this pairing could be like Sisyphus and his boulder (you can decide who is Sisyphus and who is the large stone). Just one example: as mentioned, the ISTJ is an old-fashioned sort who values traditional gender roles, so imagine a male ISTJ and a female INFP who have just gotten married. The ISTJ lays down the law: his lady must quit her job so that she can stay home to perform what he considers to be "wifely tasks," and she should be aware that that is her life from now until, well…forever. The male INFP, on the other hand, would be expected by his female ISTJ to go out there and be the breadwinner, providing for his family. That is a lot of pressure, but in both instances (for INFPs male and female) having someone expect responsibility out of them could be the positive that gives their lives direction. Ensuring that their needs are still being met in some sort of compromise with the ISTJ would be the most important factor.

2. INFP and the ISFJ

Opportunity: Because both the INFP and the ISFJ are hard-wired with similar Feeling aspects, their ability to communicate is a two-way street where information can easily flow up and down, all day long. For the INFP, having an innate understanding of what motivates the ISFJ — because they share the same motivations, which are to promote harmony and understanding — creates a decent foundation for a relationship where both sides learn to strengthen their weaknesses. INFPs can be gloriously impractical and disorganized, but because the ISFJ is a like-minded Feeling type who can communicate with sensitivity and tact, these traits could be ironed out and improved through subtle means. INFPs can look to their ISFJ counterparts and know that this more practical personality type is only trying to change them for their own benefit, so that they can be the best possible version of themselves. Meanwhile, the ISFJ might not always do so, but wen dating an INFP it can feel natural to start thinking in a way that projects toward the future and considers the possibilities of the unknown.

Threat: Perhaps the place where INFPs and ISFJs most commonly feel the tension in their differences bubble up to the surface is in the home, the location where most couples really start to learn about one another, especially right after they have moved in together. For some there is a honeymoon period of sorts, in which the neater partner overlooks the messier partner's tendency to leave dirty dishes sitting on the coffee table for days at a time (because love!), but all that blindness quickly evaporates as the reality of the situation becomes apparent. Unless INFPs really try to do otherwise, they are likely going to be that maddeningly unkempt roommate who strangely freaks out if you move their toothbrush, but who can leave a pile of clean laundry in the basket for weeks without taking the initiative to fold it and put it away. ISFJs are by nature methodical and tidy, and cleaning up after their partner — even just for weeks or months — can take its toll on the romance.

Short-term Potential: There is definite short-term potential for the INFP who finds him or herself enamored with an ISFJ. In fact, it's hard not to like this hard-working, committed and loyal personality type, especially since it is the most social and outgoing of the Introverts. INFPs might find that their own limited circle of friends expands as they become better acquainted with their ISFJ's group, but both types will still seek out those "weekends in," where they read, cook together, or watch movies — their way of re-energizing for the next event or party. INFPs might find themselves really looking up to and admiring their ISFJ partner, especially in the short-term, before all those little habits that were once cute start to drive both parties absolutely crazy. In the honeymoon stage, the INFP will look to their ISFJ and feel as though they have hit the jackpot.

Long-term Potential: Long-term relationships between these two types are tricky. They make wonderful friends, but for many, friendship isn't enough — there is a whole other layer of intimacy that most people would find absolutely essential in a long-term commitment, and that can wear off as the months and years pass by. It comes down to the way INFPs and ISFJs approach life, which are vastly different. INFPs might find that they start to feel as though they are being tethered to the ground, when all they want to do is fly. And because ISFJs like a more ordered, sensible lifestyle, INFPs can feel that no matter how hard they try to be more like their partner they are just letting them down. Some INFP/ISFJ pairings can drag on for years longer than they should, because either party is loathe to hurt the other by suggesting a break up. These Feeling types need to make sure they are talking (and listening!) to one another with open-mindedness and honesty.

3. INFP and the INFJ

Opportunity: Here is a pairing with a whole lot of understanding that goes deep, deep down. Intuitive Feelers often find that they are happiest when they are with others like them, and the matching aspects here are certainly promising. Both INFPs and INFJs are creative thinkers who could pass an entire cross-country road trip together simply by playing "What if…" suggesting to each other theoretical situations (both possible and outrageous) and raptly listening to what the other would do. This kind of imagining and positing might seem like a total waste of time to a Sensing personality, but it's a strange and wonderful fact that a game like this could bring INFPs even closer to their INFJ mate. Not only does it excite and satisfy both parties' abstract Intuitive sides, it appeals to their Feeling natures by offering insight into who they really are, underneath the surface, allowing them to communicate more fluently in both good times and bad.

Threat: Like most Introverted pairings, INFPs and INFJs have the potential to drag each other down into inactivity and unsociability, and it could be different with each pair. Perceiving INFPs might provide the kind of undisciplined personality that means to use Saturday for all the errands and home improvements but just never seems to get around to it; while INFJs are not noted for their spontaneity, and might feel that if something isn't on their to-do list, it's not getting to-done, even if it could be a lot of fun and provide an adventure to re-ignite the spark between both parties. INFPs can end up finding that, while it's wonderful to have someone "get" you on so many levels, they are bored with a Judging type who doesn't value or crave novelty in the same way. After a while, INFPs might just give up trying to take an impromptu road trip with their mate — and giving up is never a good thing when it comes to relationships.

Short-term Potential: INFPs and INFJs actually have a wonderful amount of potential when it comes to short-term relationships. Ironically, it is during the first few weeks or months that both Intuitive parties might share their dreams about where the relationship could go, picturing summer vacations together or naming their future children. The honeymoon period between these two personality types is likely to be a happy one, a blissful one even, and the type of early-stage relationship that makes you forget all rhyme or reason. INFPs shouldn't be surprised if they find themselves putting off or calling off work just so they can spend the day snuggling in bed with their new sweetie on his/her day off. It is rare for the INFP to find someone with whom they feel so compatible right away, especially because INFJs also make up a very small percentage of the population.

Long-term Potential: This duo also has some long-term potential, though it is not ideal for a few reasons. First, while the Introvert pairing can seem pretty delightful at first, after years it can get, well, kind of dull. Despite INFPs' preference for solitude or sharing the company of just a few close friends, their Perceiving aspect craves spontaneity and novelty, so once in a while a night out on the town sounds like just what the doctor ordered; yet, getting their Judging partner on board can prove to be an uphill battle. If this type of situation arises with any frequency, INFPs might end up feeling as though they are better off with someone less likely to get stuck in a rut or routine. Second, and also due to the Perceiving/Judging difference, INFPs can feel as though they are constantly being persecuted for who they are, which is a messier, less detail-oriented version of their INFJ counterpart. While the two types can easily communicate with tact and understanding, the rift in lifestyle preferences can cause lifelong misery.

4. INFP and the INTJ

Opportunity: It is always interesting when types like the INFP and the INTJ get together, because they are both creative, innovative personalities who apply their gifts in different ways, utilizing methods that one or the other would never have thought of. Even if INFPs could never naturally turn to logic and reason when they are solving a problem, dating someone who thinks that way, and with whom they communicate (and therefore have the opportunity to study), can at least give this personality type pause the next time they are faced with a crisis. While their initial reaction and ultimate decision moving forward might not be to do the thing that makes the most sense, thoughtful and introspective INFPs do have the ability (and foresight) to at least stop and consider what the outcome could be if they followed their more strategic partner's example.

Threat: Despite the fact that both types are Introverted inventors, the INFP and INTJ's approach for inventing differ radically, to the point where both parties could be working toward a common goal, like improving intimacy or ironing out a chore schedule, yet still find that there is an impossibly wide breach in their communication styles, a rift so wide that they might as well be working against each other. Both types have the imagination necessary to picture the outcome of their methods, but INTJs will always veer toward a course that emphasizes objectivity and impersonal rationality, while INFPs find that there is no more emotional situation than a relationship, and thus problems arising from said relationship should be solved by examining feelings. Judging INTJs would like to see steady and regular application of problem-solving techniques, while more free-flowing INFPs will "work on it" when they think to.

Short-term Potential: There is some short-term potential for these two types, as both types, being the Introverts they are, prefer to get very close to only a few people and will likely focus a lot of attention on each other if something brings them together (like that darn chemistry that surprisingly comes along and springs up between two people). Indeed, the sheer novelty of encountering someone who thinks so differently from them, yet with the same spark of excitement for future endeavors and possibilities, is enough to keep INFPs occupied as they analyze, in their own way, what makes the INTJ tick. It would be surprising, however, if this pairing made it past a few dates into actual relationship territory, and those couples that do have their work cut out of them.

Long-term Potential: Any long-term endeavor between these two would have to be pursued carefully, with both sides examining their feelings regularly (something INFPs could help INTJs do by nonchalantly posing questions that get them thinking about their emotions). Their Feeling/Thinking incompatibility is a great hurdle, yet it is also the source of a potential growth. If one of the most important aspects of relationship is being with someone who makes you want to be a better person, the INFP and INTJ coupledom has a lot of dynamic chemistry, but chemistry alone does not a long and happy relationship make. INFPs are going to have an incredibly difficult time relating to their INTJ mates, and this sensitive personality type might also come to find that, after years and years of emotional investment in the relationship, they feel disregarded; INTJs are known, after all, for both a brilliant intellect and a total inability to mask their derision for people who don't meet their exacting standards.

5. INFP and the ISTP

Opportunity: Despite both partners here are firmly in the Introvert camp, the world should be warned that Introvert does not equal "boring," especially when there is an ISTP thrown into the mix. INFPs, whose Perceiving aspect gives them that ethereal, otherworldly (and not likely to be happiest when confined to one corner of the world) quality can be a bit of a homebody despite some individuals' penchant for wanderlust and adventure. Enter the ISTP, who is part Indiana Jones and part MacGuyver, a singular adventurer who doesn't mind a little companionship on his or her latest jet set. For INFPs, this will be a thrilling partnership where their personal limits are tested and pushed, both in terms of physicality and emotion. What good is a relationship if you don't grow from it? Practical and self-confident ISTPs have a lot to show INFPs about what it means to explore.

Threat: There is no certainty when it will happen, but eventually the INFP might find him or herself crashing back to earth after riding high with the ISTP. Perhaps they'll run off to Morocco together for an amazing week of sunshine, exotic food and incredible sights, but when they return, the enamored INFP — looking to the future and the possibilities that exist in the years to come — might ask, "Where do you see this going?" But ISTPs, Sensing types to their fingertips, are concerned with the here and the now; what state the relationship is in a year from now never crossed their mind. In fact, it's not unlikely that they have a lover in every port of call, a discovery that would absolutely crush the INFP, who might be open-minded when it comes to love but ultimately wants commitment and loyalty at the end of the day.

Short-term Potential: The short-term potential for the INFP and the ISTP can be summed up in one word: fireworks. Active, hard-working and relentlessly mobile ISTPs are a trip to be around, and they have that dangerous edge that movie anti-heroes and femme fatales are made of. The joint Perceiving natures of the two types call out to each other, satisfied — at least momentarily — in the excitement and pleasure of finding someone else who loves new experiences and has ordered his or her life to accommodate spontaneity. For as long as the fireworks show is going, the INFPs will find themselves doing things they only wrote about with their ISTP partner, whether it's impromptu travel or reckless behavior that lands them in a foreign prison for a hot minute. But sadly, if ISTPs are the Indiana Joneses of the world, INFPs are fated to be the "leading" ladies who only exist in one film installment.

Long-term Potential: Eventually the INFP is going to demand a sit-down conversation where the two parties discuss the future of the relationship. He or she will insist that cell phones are turned off and distractions are nil. Yet the ISTP will find a way to abruptly exit the interview before everything that the INFP needs to say is said. INFPs and ISTPs just want different things when it comes to long-term relationships, and unless the ISTP has reached the point in his or her life where he or she is truly ready to settle down, the INFP — who doesn't reach the point of "settling down" easily, by any means, themselves — is doomed to be disappointed and left feeling abandoned. Again, there is a rift in the way both parties communicate, and since communication is the key component to a healthy and happy relationship, love would have little room to thrive as the thorns of suspicion, resentment, and disenchantment, particularly on the INFP's part, can spread like weeds. This is a pairing where timing is everything.

6. INFP and the ISFP

Opportunity: Ironically, one of the most beautiful things about the pairing of INFP and ISFP is how amicably they can split up and still remain friends (even best friends!). This is due in large part to their shared Feeling aspects, which will discover in one another generous and warm natures that love to give without any thought to receiving, as well as an easy rapport in the expression of thought and feeling through the arts. INFPs are renowned writers, and while ISFPs tend to dabble more in sensory, hands-on pursuits like sculpting or furniture-making, the creative impulse is alive and thriving in both, giving them much in common when it comes to understanding the need to be alone with one's thoughts and tucked away while the creative process is in progress.

Threat: Strangely, it is the commonality of Feeling aspects that can prove to be the source of conflict as well. Both parties can become slave-like in their devotion to the other, and since both types are also Introverts, their social circle — as well as their desire to go out and be around other people — is going to be rather small from the get-go. Not only does this essentially isolate them from all everyone except one another, when one type wants to go out for New Year's Eve, while the other would rather stay in and paint, real tension can arise, and both sides might be too nice to truly express how upset they are, letting resentment simmer to a boil. Further, though the ISFP is wonderfully forgiving, the INFP's penchant for living with his or her head in the clouds can supremely frustrate their grounded Sensing aspect.

Short-term Potential: INFPs paired with an ISFP in those early weeks and months will seem like a teenager in love for the very first time. As far as they are concerned, their every need and wish will be met, and all that dreaming they did of the "ideal mate" will feel as though it has sprung from their fantasies to real flesh and blood. This is a short-term pairing that might not have the fireworks of the INFP/ISTP coupling, but is instead like a walk on the beach: relaxing, romantic, gentle, and so it might last longer than most short-term relationships and will certainly have both parties swooning and gushing. Friends and family of the two types should be warned that when they find each other, they won't want to leave each other's side, so they'll either be holed up at one or another's place or insist on bringing their partner to family functions and drinks with the crew.

Long-term Potential: As blissful as the union sounds, there might not be a whole lot of growth or change between the two parties, and one or the other could eventually wake up one morning and realize that their relationship has been treading water (and someone's arms are very, very tired). If INFPs just can't seem to get their heads out of the clouds or the ISFP clings to their more traditional values as they age, friction is inevitable for this match; but on the plus side, both the INFP and the ISFP are considerate souls who would make strenuous efforts to smooth things over for as long as possible. And if a break-up is in the cards, no one will part more amicably or generously than the INFP and ISFP. They shared a life and maybe even kids — why muck up a perfectly good friendship with vengeance or pettiness?

7. INFP and the INTP

Opportunity: INFPs and INTPs have a lot in common, not the least of which is their mutual inventiveness and desire for spontaneity. If the right match is made, INFPs can find in INTP mates a great deal of like-minded creativity with an eye to the future, and instead of just dreaming about how things could be, the logical and analytical INTP can show his/her partner more concrete ways of getting things done. A lot of INFPs daydream without so much as an inkling for how to go about actually achieving their goals, but Thinking types like INTPs are more likely to put thought into deed and inspire (or outright lead) their partners into doing the same. Further, since both personalities are Perceivers, there will be little in the way of judgment if one or the other doesn't or can't see his/her latest project through.

Threat: For all that they share in terms of creativity and out-of-the-box resourcefulness, ultimately INFPs will go crazy trying to understand their Thinking partners (and vise versa), simply because these types don't feel the need to go too deep with their expression of feeling, and when they do open their mouths, they don't value tact or sensitivity the way that a Feeler very much does. So while the INFP and the INTP might be thinking the exact same thing (Pizza for dinner!), INFPs will try to coax their mate into being more communicative and open ("Come on, honey, what sounds good for dinner?") while INTPs will attempt to analyze, based on past weeks, what their mate is suggesting, never assuming it's what they are craving, too. This is a lot of dancing around and ends up wasting a great deal of time for both.

Short-term Potential: While the INFP and the INTP might not be total love birds like with other matchups, this couple still has a fairly decent shot at making it past the second date, if only because the two enjoy sharing ideas and opinions. But as with other Introverted and Thinking pairings, a duo like this left alone for longer periods of time can end up isolated, a bit bored and even kind of snippy at each other. But that's further down the road. When the INFP and the INTP are together and happy (before the honeymoon period has worn off), they can both learn a great deal about themselves — including how much patience and fortitude they have when it comes to dealing with someone who seems calibrated to think in a way that frustrates them.

Long-term Potential: INFPs and INTPs who can reach a place of mutual understanding, despite their obvious differences in motivation and decision-making, could have the ability to last a fairly long time in a committed relationship. After all, both parties love to brainstorm ideas and bounce theories off of one another, and if the chemistry is right, a little friction when it comes to their Feeling/Thinking aspects could be a lifelong learning experience. Then there's the fact that both personalities crave novelty and dismiss the mundane, the banal and ties that bind them to a place or a job. As long as that "dream vacation" actually becomes a reality now and then, these dedicated Introverts can keep the spark alive for the long haul. They must simply make honest communication and dedicated action priorities in their shared lives, so that they don't waste too much time thinking and not doing.

8. INFP and the ESTP

Opportunity: As overwhelming as ESTP personalities can be, INFPs are an interesting foil to this more outgoing type, tempering them and giving them cause to pause before leaping into action (and perhaps even saving them from themselves). Yet INFPs are clearly spontaneous themselves, so their advice is less likely to come off as judgmental or critical. In fact, the INFP might show the ESTP a thing or two in the variety-is-the-spice-of-life category, offering up a pleasant (and shocking) surprise now and then to an Extraverted personality type who thinks he/she can tell everything just by looking at someone. In return, ESTPs get the Introverted INFPs off the couch or away from the laptop and out meeting people, face-to-face, like the good old days, an activity the INFP can definitely use more practice in.

Threat: The INFP and the ESTP diverge in two major areas. First, the INFP likes to think about ideas, theories and the possibilities of the future, whereas the ESTP takes a grounded, practical, and straightforward approach to dating. Second, Feeling INFPs in arguments are bound to tiptoe around what they really want to say, whereas the less tactful ESTP is perfectly comfortable just coming out and telling it like it is. This usually ends with the INFPs having their feelings hurt, and it can lead to them withdrawing to lick to their wounds for a few days. By the time they decide to return their ESTP's text, they might find that their mile-a-minute companion has found someone else to warm his/her heart (and bed), and this new person has a refreshing bluntness that the INFP lacks.

Short-term Potential: Without a doubt, there will be thrilling passion between the INFP and the ESTP in the early stage of a relationship, as the ESTP's warm sensuality is met and perhaps even exceeded by the INFP's open-mindedness and creativity in the boudoir. ESTPs usually have a lot on their plate, and it may titillate both parties to have this personality type come running home to his/her INFP between obligations for a delightful tryst. Even in a short period of time the INFP's Feeling aspect can be quite infectious, and so despite a very brief time between the conception of the relationship and it's expiration, the INFP's loving and giving nature can teach even this analytical and less mindful personality type what it means to show someone you really care.

Long-term Potential: Like all glowing things that run on battery power, the relationship between an INFP and an ESTP will probably burn out in the long run unless both parties can really make the effort to push forward. Though Introvert/Extravert pairings tend to be more successful over the long term, in this instance the core aspects of Intuitive vs. Sensing and Feeling vs. Thinking might be too different to allow these mutual free spirits to forge a lasting bond that can weather the storms that accompany commitments like marriage and children. An inability to communicate in a meaningful and successful way could be the ultimate nail in the coffin, but if both the INFP and the ESTP are willing to put in the effort to find a happy medium the excitement of the early days might endure. If not, INFPs will emerge from this pairing a little bit wiser and a little bit more cautious about giving their hearts away.

9. INFP and the ESFP

Opportunity: One of the best things about this pretty wonderful pairing is how beautifully the two types are able to communicate. The thing that most couples need to talk about more, particularly in the beginning stages, is where each person stands with each other, and that's a topic that scares off a lot of people. Normally you would think INFPs and ESFPs, because they are both Perceiving types, would rather back away from that subject, but actually, among the many things they enjoy discussing is the fact that both parties would prefer to take their time when it comes to finding someone to settle down with (in fact, both types might know this from experience, after rushing into previous relationships and finding that was not the best course of action). Security in the "standing" of their relationship opens the door to both types just being able to enjoy each other's company and all the wonderful experiences they can share.

Threat: Although INFPs will feel comfortable expressing when they simply do not want to accompany their more outgoing partners for a night out on the town, meeting and mingling in bars or at friends' house parties, it can become a real drag if the ESFPs are doing what they do — trying to convince their favorite person to come enjoy life with them. Further, INFPs like to think and theorize about the future and all the richness of possibilities, while ESFPs want to leap before they look and just go out and do things without much forethought. While this pairing has excellent prospects for communication and understanding, no one is perfect and no couple can be together without the little arguments and tiffs that make us human.

Short-term Potential: The short-term potential for this match-up is quite good, probably beginning with the ESFP being his or her natural outgoing self and asking out the INFP with a typical nonchalance. INFPs, being a creatures who keep to themselves most commonly, will likely be flattered that someone so popular and magnetic has expressed an interest in them, and the two will quickly form an attachment while sensibly keeping each other at arm's length initially. The early weeks and months are an action-packed yet emotional time when ESFPs induce INFPs to join them at parties and events, while staying sensitive to their Introverted date's need for solitude as replenishment.

Long-term Potential: The INFP and the ESFP have excellent long-term potential, despite the fact that one thinks Intuitively while the other is Sensing. Because both types are naturally sensitive and understanding, they can communicate easily and effectively. Their differences in Intuitiveness/Sensing act as foils rather than relationship spoils, so that the dreamy INFPs learn over time the finer points of more practical and direct thinking (perhaps they will finally comprehend the importance of getting an oil change on time), while the ESFP sees what it's like to dream big and consider how a single action can have multiple possible outcomes. The two further complement each other with their similar Perceiving aspects, so that a messy living room doesn't breed lifelong resentment and both parties stay open-minded to change throughout their lives together.

10. INFP and the ENFP

Opportunity: Now, it depends on each individual pairing of these two types, but the vast majority of INFP and ENFP couples are going to be in a really good place for as long as they are together. You might not think it, but the Introvert/Extravert dynamic is just what each type needs to have one of the happiest, healthiest and longest-enduring relationships of their lives — in fact, this couple has the possibility of being each other's One Great Love. Aside from how the differences in energy levels (and from whence each type gets their energy) complement one another, the sameness of the rest of their personality aspects work in fantastic ways, too. Both sides are generous and loving, affectionate and imaginative, and neither type is going to get worked up if he/she comes home from work and finds that the living room is messy.

Threat: There is not a whole lot that can go wrong for the INFP who is matched up with an ENFP, except that there is not a whole lot of potential for growth. Granted, the more Extraverted ENFPs can certainly get their retiring counterpart to learn how to appreciate a little social energy over staying in for too many weekends in a row, but other than that, the two types are so alike that they might find themselves a touch bored or even dismayed at how they have been together for years and yet neither type has a salaried job (because they never felt the pressure to get one — it's always live wild and free with the INFP/ENFP). This prevents them from doing things like truly settling down, buying a house, maybe even starting a family. Not that that's everyone's path in life, but while INFPs in particular might take a while to find their "settling down" partner, these types do desire a fulfilling long-term relationship with all the bells and whistles.

Short-term Potential: Obviously the short-term potential for this match-up is great, and the beginning of the relationship is going to be one of the most exciting and exuberant times in either party's life. It is incredibly rare that we find someone who verges on soulmate status, but these two definitely have that potential. INFPs and ENFPs view the world in the most similar of ways, and they will find themselves staying up all night talking about their hopes and dreams for the future. They will find that, time and again, they finish each other's sentences or end up reading the same books without discussing it first. If you have ever had a relationship like this, then you know that finding someone who makes you feel like you are looking in the mirror is a heady, emotional experience that produces a rush better than any drug.

Long-term Potential: The long-term potential for these two is excellent, and while that aforementioned rush of emotions might make this spontaneous duo run away and elope after a few months, they have the right combination of personality traits to defy the odds (and all the naysayers) with a lasting, loving, and loyal relationship that spans the decades. When these two look at each other at their 50th wedding anniversary, everyone will still see stars in their eyes. The one matter of contention with this pairing is their joint Perceiving aspects, which means that both of them shy away from settling with a steady job and both of them seek out novelty and new experiences. This works in the short-term and may be a part of each other that strengthens their bond, but in the long-term, without someone having the natural inclination for an anchor in their life, both the INFP and the ENFP can find themselves adrift and aimless, not reaching their full capacity for achievement.

11. INFP and the ENTP

Opportunity: The INFP will have to make great efforts in understanding their Thinking counterpart, the ENTP, but if this latter type can also reach out and try to meet him/her in the middle where communication is concerned then this matchup could provide some interesting lessons and potential for personal growth. The INFP and the ENTP will at least find common ground when it comes to their enthusiasm for future endeavors, whether it's creative pursuits or work-related concepts that they haven't shared with anyone else for fear of being judged or laughed at, and both types won't get upset or take it personally if they set a date and time for dinner and one or the other is late.

Threat: Normally an Introversion/Extraversion pairing provides the right kind of contrast in personality so that neither is homebound for too long nor runs the risk of burning the other out from too much marathon partying. But in this instance, where the ENTP's Extraversion is paired with a Thinking aspect, the results are less than desirable, because Thinkers are notoriously blunt and insensitive — and while they might be so under their breath as an Introvert, Extraverts have no notion of what "under the breath" means; they'll just come right out and say whatever they're thinking, and sorry if your feelings got hurt! This is just too frank for the INFP, who is a gentle nurturer with a rather surprising capacity for lashing out when he/she feels threatened.

Short-term Potential: There is some short-term potential for this couple, although the sparks will fly early on. That can provide just the right kind of chemistry that the INFP and the ENTP need when it comes to a physical relationship, but unfortunately the Feeling and Thinking aspects are going to scrape against each other in the worst way, compounded by the ENTP's outgoing (and some would say overbearing) personality, which always has to be the center of attention. Both sides will feel as though they are "putting up with" the other, and they might find themselves staying together because they see good stuff in the other, and they both hope that things will work themselves out as time goes on. But without a strong communication base, matters most certainly will not fix themselves, and even if the INFP and ENTP can find a way to talk to one another, it will still be an uphill struggle to understand each other's motivations and values.

Long-term Potential: While there is potential for personal growth, INFPs and ENTPs have a very difficult battle ahead of them when it comes to relating to one another in a way that allows them to constructively teach each other about their opposing points of view. The ENTP will have to learn how to back off and let the INFP sort out his/her feelings, while the INFP must develop a stronger voice and not be as hesitant to speak up, especially when something is bothering him/her (perhaps one of the best things about Thinking types is how little they take offense when someone offers critique!). If the INFP and ENTP can find a middle ground, they will be able to listen to each other's ideas throughout their lives together and grow in love and appreciation for the other's gifts.

12. INFP and the ESTJ

Opportunity: Perhaps the INFP will show up at his/her next family reunion in a nice outfit and be able to tell everyone how he/she landed a really great job with a firm who occupies office space at the top of a skyscraper. Grandma and Grandpa will be so pleased, but they'll be shocked that their wayward free-spirit of a grandchild is suddenly joining the corporate world, giving up meat, and starting to do yoga. Chalk it up to the influence of his/her ESTJ significant other, one of the most traditional and assertive personality types on the MBTI spectrum and a veritable sentinel of decorum and values. There really is no telling how these two ended up together, but one thing is for certain: the ESTJ would take one look at the INFP's life and immediately set about improving it with the best of intentions, lining up job interviews at places that actually have health benefits and getting them on an exercise regimen.

Threat: And all of that effort, even if it comes from the bottom of the ESTJ's heart, is going to be met with some pretty fierce opposition, even if doesn't come up right away. For a time, the ESTJ can convince the INFP that he/she needs to make some responsible changes to his/her life, but INFPs will eventually (and this is probably sooner, rather than later) realize that this is hogwash and they like their life the way it was. While the sweetly Feeling INFPs will agonize over the most diplomatic way to completely reject the ESTJ's efforts, it is more likely that they will reach a boiling point and froth over, blowing up with uncharacteristic but utterly passionate assertion (taking gardening shears to their new business suit sounds about right). And ultimately, that will be that.

Short-term Potential: Because INFPs are so accommodating and can get swept up in the authority of someone more assertive than they, there is some likelihood that they can assume a submissive position under the ESTJ and a relationship could work for a few weeks or even months. After all, INFPs like novelty, and if their last significant other was more like them, going off in the complete other direction in terms of personality can be exciting and interesting. As open-minded and flexible individuals, INFPs like trying on different lifestyles to see what fits, and there is a good chance they have never donned the ESTJ's mode of living — but INFPs are no fools, they can definitely see the benefits of a grounded career and sound financial investments. They might even start daydreaming in typical INFP fashion about how their life with the ESTJ looks years down the road, a beautiful home, white picket fence, 2.5 children, and a dog.

Long-term Potential: If this is really what the INFP wants, he/she is going to have to make serious sacrifices to see it through. ESTJs are devoted traditionalists who have no qualms about impressing their views and opinions on all who come into their sphere, and that most certainly includes their romantic partners. Perhaps the view that will cause the INFP the most cause for dismay is the ESTJ's belief in traditional gender spheres, where the man works outside the home and "brings home the bacon," while the woman stays home to clean, cook and mind the children. It could scare off INFPs to find that they have a "role" expected of them within the confines of their relationship with the ESTJ, but some INFPs will reach the point in their lives — after living enough for 10 people — where what they truly want is the stability and financial security that ESTJs can offer. It would be an adjustment, for sure, but if the INFP is happy, then a long marriage can be expected.

13. INFP and the ESFJ

Opportunity: The Extraversion + Feeling aspects of the ESFJ combine to make this type a warm, loving and compassionate personality with whom the INFP will feel an immediate connection. The SFJ combination in particular denotes a bubbly, social, and popular kind of person (the Introverted ISFJ is the most outgoing type of all the Introverts), and the gentle, sensitive way that he or she approaches others will appeal to the INFP, who will likely find him or herself being drawn out of isolation and engaging in more social activities than ever before (and not hating it or counting down the moments until he/she can go home!). In return, the thoughtful and contemplative INFPs can help ESFJs learn how to slow down a bit, enjoy a quiet evening in and be comfortable when they are alone with just their thoughts for company.

Threat: There will be some tension in terms of how the INFP and ESFJ approach their lives together, especially since the ESFJ is and always has been looking for someone to marry and have kids with. It's not that INFPs don't want that — most of them truly do, but they prefer to wait and make sure that the person they are with is really the one with whom they want to share that experience. It's typical Intuitive vs. Sensing friction, and it can cause both sides a lot of heartache, especially if they have come to care about each other and have invested a lot emotionally in the relationship. INFPs might feel as though they are being rushed into making a decision about their future, while the ESFJ is looking at the clock, thinking, "Time is slipping away! All we have is now!"

Short-term Potential: INFPs and ESFJs have the potential for a very satisfying short-term relationship, and this is one matchup where the two personalities are able to communicate and, therefore, learn from one another. Even in a matter of months, the ESFJ can show the INFP how important the family unit is and how meaningful and special it is to build a life with someone else, making the INFP's less established ways seem even more immature and irresponsible in contrast. This pairing could be a very important step in the INFP's path toward real adulthood, so that even if he or she is not ready yet, the seed has been planted and this person knows what kind of person to look for in the years ahead, when it becomes more attractive to him/her to get married and have kids.

Long-term Potential: In the happiest of instances, the INFP and the ESFJ will meet at just the right time, when the INFP is finally ready to settle down and the ESFJ hasn't reached that frenzied place in their life when they are wildly desperate to get married (that kind of desperation is going to be a huge turn-off to the INFP and might push them in the opposite direction, toward wanting more freedom!). If they do happen to come across one another at this "sweet spot" in their lives, the potential for a beautiful and lasting marriage is definitely present. But like solar eclipses, the celestial bodies have to align just right, and the likelihood is that these two types will not meet at a time that is complementary for them both. They will truly enjoy each other's company, though, and take away from the relationship a whole store of lessons, memories and perhaps even some regret.

14. INFP and the ENFJ

Opportunity: Without a doubt, this match has the potential to be the most earth-shattering and life-affirming of all the pairings for the INFP. Those matching NF functions mean that both types have similar worldviews — looking to the future, appreciating the abstract/theoretical, and treating others with the compassion and kindness with which they would want to be treated — while the "opposing" traits aren't really at odds at all. The solid foundation of understanding that exists between the INFP and the ENFJ enables them to learn from each other, oftentimes without even realizing it, and become the very best versions of themselves that they can be. While ENFJs are outgoing and unafraid of being assertive when they need to, they are gentle enough to bring INFPs out of their shells gradually, showing them how forging good interpersonal relationships is both useful and emotionally fulfilling.

Threat: There is very little threat of tension or major argument — enough to break them up — between the INFP and the ENFJ, and that's not even when both parties are on their best behavior. They are both simply hard-wired to be kind and considerate to others, and they will turn that toward each other, with the volume pumped up. But if there is anything that could get this pairing off track, it's the fact that neither wants the other to be unhappy, so these types will either bend over backward trying to please their partner (without regard to their own needs) or avoid confrontation and the necessary conversation that needs to happen, simply because it could be unpleasant and make both partners upset for who knows how long. While any problem, if left unaddressed for too long, can blossom into a relationship-ending issue, the openness of the INFP and ENFJ relationship should be more than enough to overcome any obstacle or disagreement.

Short-term Potential: The short-term potential of the INFP and ENFJ relationship is as excellent as you would expect, but it's is interesting that INFPs might not initially expect themselves to work so well with ENFJs.

ENFJs are comfortable in crowds, after all, happy to share chit-chat with all of their many acquaintances, and they are much more grounded in their personal and professional lives, willing to commit to buying a house and working a 9-to-5 where they are expected to show up on time, every day. But the genuine warmth which exists with both types, combined with their wondrous approach to the world, where nothing is exactly as it seems, will make it blindingly obvious to INFPs that this is someone with whom they can and should stick around for a while to see where the relationship goes. While ESTJs are going to order them to improve their life, ENFJs teach by example, showing their counterpart how good it can be to not only embrace a more settled lifestyle but to be with someone who wants to help them achieve it.

Long-term Potential: Of all the pairings, this one has the most potential to go the distance. This is the coupling that will end only when both parties have returned to dust, the Great Love that cannot be replaced in one another's hearts, even if one passes and the other remarries. Few of us ever have the opportunity to be with someone who understands us a little more each day (while always having little surprises in store to keep thing interesting) and who makes us better people without even trying. But that is the ultimate takeaway with the INFP and ENFJ couple, and things will never be boring when there is enough of a difference between the two so that they will always have things to learn from one another — like how to relax and show a little spontaneity, where the ENFJ is concerned, or the value of an organized junk drawer, for the INFP — while maintaining the same core values.

15. INFP with the ENTJ

Opportunity: Because the INFP and the ENTJ both have well-developed Intuitive aspects, a relationship between the two could be both challenging and entertaining (at least at first). ENTJs are well known for being planners, and if they find someone they like, they will focus that energy on making each date special and exciting (perhaps even spending a great deal of their hard-earned money to impress), something the more laid-back INFPs will certainly appreciate and take into account when they consider their feelings on how the date went, long after it has ended. While both types are in the beginning phases of feeling one another out, perhaps the ENTJs will let their guard down enough to allow the INFP to show them how a less structured approach to life isn't as bad as they had imagined; the ENTJs might even begin to imagine how things could be if they stuck with the INFPs and absorbed some of their spontaneity once in a while.

Threat: Still, the friction between the INFP and the ENTJ has the potential to overwhelm the good stuff. ENTJs are natural-born leaders who like to issue orders and see them carried out with efficiency, while INFPs have spent their lives dodging the types of situations where people are seriously depending on them with stringent time restraints and high expectations. INFPs' lackadaisical approach to life — which they love and wouldn't change for the world if they are happy and thriving — will come across as seriously immature to the ENTJ, who works hard everyday, doing things like conquering the corporate world or overseeing major business mergers before returning home to his/her million-dollar condo (that the ENTJ definitely owns). ENTJs are going to appear straight-laced and uptight to the INFP, while the latter type is going to look like an irresponsible drifter, and those are tough differences to overcome when both types are set in their ways.

Short-term Potential: If there is any short-term potential for these two types, it's mostly of the fun, non-serious variety. Although the ENTJ tends to plan for the future (a cut-and-run kind of person when he/she senses that the relationship isn't going anywhere) the INFP is such an intriguing blend of free-spiritedness and lack of pretention that the ENTJ might stick around just for the heck of it. The ENTJ does, after all, have a surprisingly amount of versatility and flexibility when it comes to intimate matters, and that is a trait which will be very appealing to the imaginative and expressive INFP, who prefers those intimate one-on-one times to big parties or loud clubs. The INFPs will be content to wait at home, perhaps working on their novel in bed, until their more outgoing partner returns home to them after a social gathering.

Long-term Potential: When an Extraverted Thinker is paired with an Introverted Feeler, the outcome is a challenging one, because the way they interact with each other will always be at odds; louder, more brash Extraverts who have the typical Thinking frankness are a rude awakening for quieter Introverts that have always relied on their sensitive Feeling aspect to treat people with tact and courtesy. Couples can, of course, through therapy and other means, work on improving communication skills and methods — for instance, INFPs might find that writing out their concerns to their ENTJ mate is an effective way to get their point across without becoming hyperemotional on the spot. The ENTJ could then respond in kind or speak face-to-face, but what matters is that the Extravert takes the time to choose his/her words carefully. If the INFP means enough to them, it will be worth it for the ENTJs to make the effort — and they will get better with practice.

Printed in Great Britain
by Amazon.co.uk, Ltd.,
Marston Gate.